SALISBURY ILLUSTRATED

The City's Heritage in Prints and Drawings

Alan W. Ball

HALSGROVE

For Marion

First published in 2000 by Halsgrove
Copyright © 2000, Alan W. Ball

ISBN 1 84114 076 7

British Library Cataloguing-in-Publication-Data
A CIP data for this book is available from the British Library

HALSGROVE
Halsgrove House
Lower Moor Way
Tiverton EX16 6SS
T: 01884 243242
F: 01884 243325
www.halsgrove.com

Printed and bound in Great Britain
by MPG Ltd, Bodmin

CONTENTS

The monument to Sir Thomas Gorges in the retrochoir of the Cathedral. This splendid and highly mannerist piece of work looks as if it were commissioned from a pattern book of ornaments. Obelisks, polyhedra, the Four Virtues and columns like sticks of barley sugar, all combine to dazzle the eye. Sir Thomas designed the curiously triangular Longford Castle as his residence and would doubtless have approved of his monument, had he been able to see it. The etching dated 1 June 1815 is by John Le Keux from a drawing by T. Baxter and comes from John Britton's *Cathedral Antiquities* (230x170).

GENERAL INTRODUCTION

At first glance Salisbury seems to have little in common with Stevenage, Telford, Peterlee, the area north of Princes Street in Edinburgh or Winchelsea. All six places however are new towns built originally on green field sites. Salisbury and Winchelsea are thirteenth-century foundations laid out on a grid pattern like the bastides of south-western France. These latter were constructed in this way so that troops could be moved easily for defence from one point to another, especially in the Hundred Years War, while Winchelsea was rebuilt on a different site when the previous town was overwhelmed by the sea in a great storm. A modified form of grid was used in Salisbury, presumably because it was so much easier than creating a haphazard series of curving streets with more complicated sites for houses and shops. The late eighteenth-century grid of Edinburgh New Town had of course a totally different style of buildings, but the same principles were at work. By contrast the post Second World War new towns tended to have many more curved streets and crescents to create an informal atmosphere.

However, the grid used by the planners in Salisbury had to be modified to accommodate existing roads coming in from the outside and to direct a good supply of water through the area in open conduits down the centre of streets. These had small bridges or crossing places to give people and horses and carts easy access. Originally this was to allow a sufficient supply of sweet water, which had been so scarce at Old Sarum, but by the eighteenth century Daniel Defoe in his *Tour Through the Whole Island of Great Britain* was writing: 'Salisbury itself is indeed a large and pleasant city, though I do not think it all the pleasanter for that which they boast so much of, namely, the water running through the middle of every street, or that it adds anything to the beauty of the place, but just the contrary, it keeps the streets always dirty, full of wet and filth and weeds, even in the middle of summer.' The less salubrious washing processes of the woollen trade, for which Salisbury had been famous since as early as the fourteenth or fifteenth centuries, had by then quite clearly created little more than open sewers on the model of the Fleet Ditch in London.

In one way when the planners of New Salisbury left Old Sarum they created two new towns, as the Close was part of the new City, but at the same time a quite separate area around the Cathedral. The laying out of the City went hand in hand with the construction of the Cathedral and Close and gave Salisbury that very special atmosphere, which it still retains in large measure to this day.

There were of course many visitors in addition to Defoe, who came to the City and recorded their impressions. William Worcestre was a confidential clerk living in genteel poverty, who occasionally broke out and went on drunken binges, after which he had to borrow money from his friends. He was in Salisbury in August 1478 and coming in from the south-east was sober enough to be full of admiration for this view of the City. John Leland the antiquary was a visitor in 1537. He admired the Cathedral and added 'There are many fair streets in the City of Salisbury, especially the High Street and Castle Street'. William Schellinks, a Dutch merchant, observed on a visit in 1662 that 'There is a most magnificent Cathedral or main church with a very tall pointed spire and two transepts'. He also noted that there were at least 70 inns for the accommodation of travellers and as many ale houses in addition.

Samuel Pepys, that archetypal urban man, came to the City in June 1668 and was greatly frightened by being on Old Sarum at night, but by way of compensation he stayed at 'The George Inn, where I lay in a silk bed and very good diet'. Sadly there is no record of his usual amorous pursuits, either with chambermaids or ladies higher up the social scale. That indomitable horsewoman Celia Fiennes came in the last two decades of the same century and left enthusiastic descriptions of the City, as did Arthur Young, the keen agriculturalist in 1767.

John Evans, the self-styled 'Juvenile Tourist' was a visitor in the first decade of the nineteenth century and admired Salisbury, but seemed much more taken with a tour of Wilton House. William Cobbett was at his usual ill-tempered best in August 1826 when he characterised Old Sarum as 'that accursed hill', presumably from its having a history as a rotten borough returning two members of parliament. From there he descended into the City, which he described as being a very miserable place and attended a service in a transept of the Cathedral. This consisted of only nine people and 'a parson of some sort with a white covering on him'. Cobbett admired the building, but fulminated against the clergy in general as being part of a conspiracy to take bread out of the mouths of poor labourers.

At the end of the nineteenth century there were a number of American visitors. Henry James in his *English Hours* of 1875 regarded the Cathedral as being almost too perfect and the architectural equivalent of 'flaxen hair and blue eyes physionomically'. This description puts it almost in the category of the rather helpless heroines of many of the early silent films. The artist Joseph Pennell was a Quaker and was in the City in July and August 1885 producing illustrations for Mrs Schuyler Van Rensselaer's *English Cathedrals*. He likened the Purbeck marble shafts in the Cathedral to the down pipes of a typical heating system in a New England Friends' Meeting House and characterised the Dean and Canons as 'the most beautiful, useless ornaments of England'. On the other hand there was nothing but praise from another American visitor, Anna Bowman Dodd in her *Cathedral Days* of 1887, although she had a distressing habit of seeing quaintness everywhere.

There were of course in addition many artists who visited the City, chief among them being Constable and Turner. However it is not the aim of this work to deal with original paintings or the multitude of photographic images of the City, but rather with the copper, steel and wood engravings, etchings and line drawings commissioned to illustrate books and periodicals. Many of the artists and process workers in these media barely scraped a tolerable living, but they have left behind a fascinating picture of Salisbury, which will remain bright and fresh when the prose they enhanced is all but forgotten. As these prints and engravings often appear at a different size from the originals, I have indicated the real dimensions in millimetres in brackets at the end of each caption with the height first and width second. In addition, because there is much detail that is likely to elude the naked eye, it is recommended that a magnifying glass is used to bring into sharper focus the more obscure parts of the illustrations.

Finally it should be made clear that there is such as wealth of suitable material available, it has only been possible to include a carefully chosen selection, and I can only apologise in advance if many of your favourite illustrations have not been included.

A stone capital from the arcade round the Cathedral chapter house. The artist is James Kellaway Colling and it comes from volume two of his work entitled *Gothic Ornaments* of 1850. The lithographer is J.R. Jobbins and the date of this particular illustration September 1848. As well as being a trained architect, Colling was a noted water-colourist with a strong interest in producing illustrations of natural forms and foliage and there is a selection of his work in the R.I.B.A. Drawings Collection (165x160).

OLD SARUM

If you were choosing a site for a Cathedral, it would hardly seem sensible to select a windy hilltop. However, when the Normans conquered England, they set about constructing castles to control their new realm and replacing Saxon ministers with imposing and magnificent cathedrals. It is therefore not surprising that castle and cathedral grew up together with the town to service them on a height that had commanded such a sweep of countryside from Britain's earliest history. As time passed, tensions arose between the divergent needs of the military and ecclesiastical authorities, until finally the problem was only resolved by the construction of a new Cathedral and City from 1219 onwards near the confluence of the Rivers Avon and Nadder. As the population moved down to the new City in the valley below and the need for a castle declined, Old Sarum gradually became the preserve of the agriculturalist and pastoralist and a place of desolation, especially in stormy weather.

The final indignity was for the whole area to become in effect a stone quarry to help with the new construction in the city that replaced it. Thus the building of the early medieval castle, cathedral and town on this strategic height proved to be an extremely short chapter in the long sequence of its previous human occupation.

A view of Old Sarum by Charles E. Flower from E.E. Dorling's *History of Salisbury* of 1911. The fields below the heights have stooked grain, a sight now long since vanished from the agricultural scene (50x125).

William Stukeley was appointed Secretary to the Society of Antiquaries in 1717 and in 1724 published his *Itinerarium Curiosem*. This sketch of Old Sarum dated 1 August 1723 is taken from that work and makes the hill-fort look rather like a large and imposing flying saucer. Cobbett on the other hand thought it appeared to be three cheeses of differing sizes piled one on top of the other. Salisbury appears on the right dominated by its Cathedral and so the viewpoint must be in a south-westerly direction from the City (150x270).

Two mezzotints of Old Sarum by David Lucas after John Constable. These powerful works pushed Lucas to the very limits of his technical ability. That above was issued in part two of Constable's *English Landscape Scenery* of 1830, while the one (right) is from the second edition of 1833. Constable had always been moved by the thought of a once thriving city, castle and cathedral being transformed into a hill top desolation open to the winds and storms of heaven, a mood that was markedly accentuated by the death of his wife Maria in 1828, his old friend Archdeacon John Fisher in August 1832 and his erstwhile painting assistant Johnny Dunthorne in November of the same year (both 150x220).

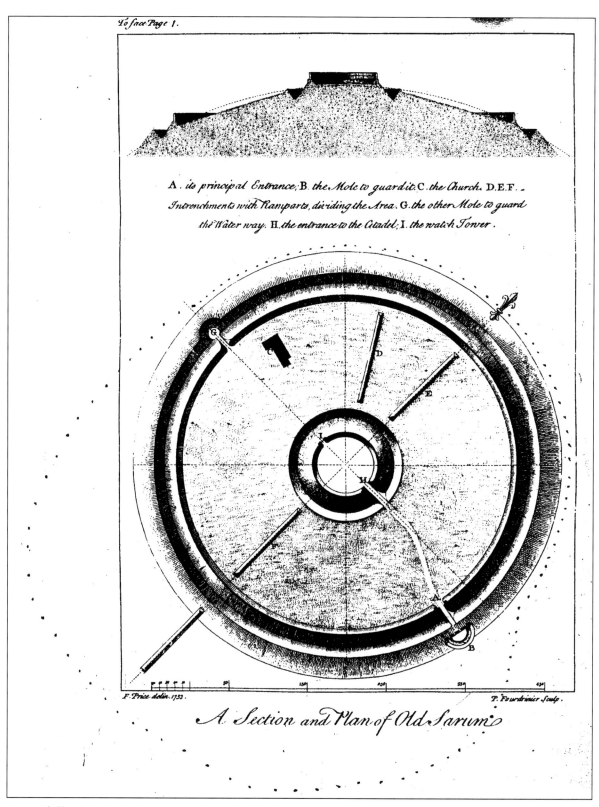

A. its principal Entrance; B. the Mole to guard it; C. the Church. D.E.F.
Intrenchments with Ramparts, dividing the Area. G. the other Mole to guard
the Water way. H. the entrance to the Citadel; I. the watch Tower.

F. Price delin. 1753.

T. Fourdrinier Sculp.

A Section and Plan of Old Sarum

A carefully detailed plan and section of Old Sarum
by Francis Price from his *A Series of Observations on
the Cathedral Church of Salisbury* of 1753 (235x175).

An attractive engraving after a drawing by J. Fisher showing a near view of Old Sarum across fields. There is a farmhouse in the near distance and a landscape stretching away on the left, while various people walk about on pathways and a shepherd chats to a lounging friend with sheep and a dog in attendance. The view comes from Peter Hall's *Picturesque Memorials of Salisbury* of 1834 (90x175).

This sketch by Herbert Railton is entitled *Old Sarum from the Devizes Road* and comes from Richard le Gallienne's *Travels in England* of 1900 (55x110).

A similar view of Old Sarum to those on the previous page. The artist is Bernard C. Gotch and it comes from a 1910 edition of W.H. Hudson's *A Shepherd's Life* (85x155).

Two anonymous engravings of Old Sarum from Thomas Wright's *Wanderings of an Antiquary* of 1854. That above is a south-westerly view from the Devizes Road and the one below from Little Durnford Hill, roughly from a northerly direction with the spire of the Cathedral on the right and the tower of Stratford sub Castle Church, farther to the right (both 55x100).

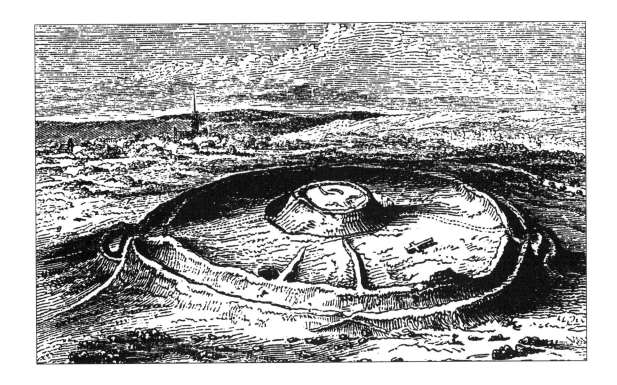

Four more anonymous engravings of Old Sarum from Thomas Wright's *Wanderings of an Antiquary* of 1854, which are similar to those on the previous page. Above a bird's-eye view, with Salisbury on the left (55x95). Below left the eastern entrance with Salisbury in the distance on the left (55x90). Below right an outer entrenchment (45x65). Bottom a section of walling (50x100).

DISTANT VIEWS

alisbury is supremely lucky in that most of the roads into the City provide at some point magical views of the distant Cathedral spire and the town around it. From the south over Harnham Hill the Downs and Old Sarum form a remote and rather bleak background, from Wilton in the west there is a more intimate and domestic approach, while the eastern roads from Andover and Southampton and the northern entry from Amesbury provide their own delights. It is better not to prefer one to the other, but to enjoy them all in changing lights and seasons.

Cosmo the third, Grand Duke of Tuscany, made a visit to the south of England in 1669, which was something of a royal progress. The Duke was received as an honoured guest in the houses of the nobility and gentry and his travels were issued as a publication by J. Mawman in this country in 1821. This work has views adapted by Thomas Hosmer Shepherd from those produced by an artist in the Grand Duke's entourage. The one of Salisbury resembles nothing so much as parts assembled from a child's toy box and is dated 1 January 1821. The sepia aquatinting of the plates after the Italian artist's original work must have been a somewhat strange commission for Thomas Hosmer Shepherd, who is much better known for his London views (145x265).

A similar view to the one above by William Stukeley from his *Itinerarium Curiosem* of 1724 with Old Sarum on the extreme left. It is entitled *View from Harnham Hill* and the trees in this well-wooded scene have the curious air of a line of troops drawn up for inspection. This engraving is dated 26 August 1723 (150x260).

A north-east view of the City as Naish saw it in 1751, but reworked by J. Fisher for Peter Hall's *Picturesque Memorials of Salisbury* of 1834. The spire of St Martin's church is on the extreme left, followed by the Cathedral in the centre, still with its detached bell tower removed by James Wyatt in 1790. Then in order come St Thomas' church, St Edmund's church (now an arts centre) and in the distance on the far right St Clement's church, Fisherton, demolished in 1852 and replaced by the present church of St Paul. There is a great deal of activity going on with a waggon, carriage and pedestrians on the left, three figures taking a breather in the centre and what at first glance appear to be two curiously shaped poles on the right hand path ahead of the small line of trees. These must be women with baskets on their heads filled with produce to sell in the market (85x180).

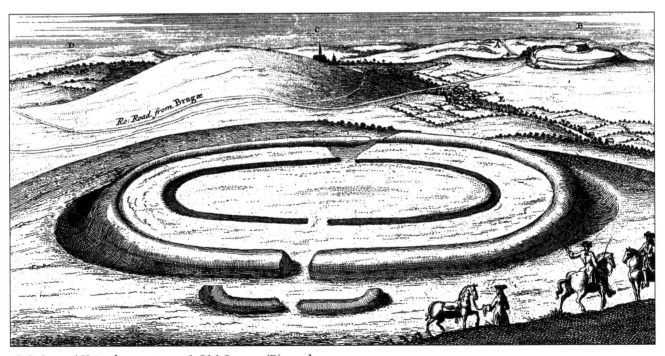

Salisbury (C) in the centre and Old Sarum (B) on the extreme right from Figsbury Ring. A north-easterly view with Ford (E) and the wooded area covering the scantiest remains of a once medieval royal palace at Clarendon (D). This view is from William Stukeley's *Itinerarium Curiosem* of 1724 (145x270).

The spire of the Cathedral is visible on the horizon on the extreme left in this sketch of Old Sarum by Nelly Erichsen. It comes from *Highways and Byways in Wiltshire*, written by Edward Hutton before the First World War, but not published until 1917 (95x80).

The spire of the Cathedral shows as a tiny white mark just breaking the horizon on the left in this view of Salisbury from Old Sarum. The two sets each of two figures, one in the foreground and the other on the ridge in the distance guide the eye onwards towards the distant objective. The artist and engraver is James Sargant Storer and the view comes from Volume 4 of his *History and Antiquities of the Cathedral Churches of Great Britain* of 1819 (78x115).

A north-eastern view of the City from the *European Magazine* dated 1 October 1805 entitled *Salisbury from the London Road*. The artist is John Nixon and the engraver Samuel Rawle, St Edmund's church (now an arts centre) stands between the Cathedral and the two rustic figures in deep conversation in the foreground. The depiction of the spire has been considerably exaggerated to produce a more dramatic effect (85x140).

A pastoral south-west view of Salisbury engraved by Thomas Higham from a drawing by George Fennel Robson and dated 1 March 1827. It comes from John Britton's *Picturesque Views of the English Cities*, also of 1827. This had no text to avoid the need for legal deposit and as only one thousand copies were printed it is now extremely rare. Robson was born in Durham and painted extensively, but not exclusively, in Scotland and the north of England (135x225).

This anonymous, but extremely detailed and powerful wood-engraved south-western view of the City comes from the *Illustrated London News* of 31 August 1872. The tower of St Thomas' church is to the left of the Cathedral, that of St Edmund's church (now an arts centre) standing up above the Cathedral roof with St Martin's church and its spire on the extreme right (290x415).

One of the perils of changing from a hill-top site like Old Sarum to the present well-watered Salisbury of today is the danger of flooding. The medium of wood engraving proves to be a perfect way of capturing the misery and gloom engendered by the floods of 1852 and 1883. The anonymous artists for the *Illustrated London News* have even managed to make the willows look pathetic and dejected. The view above is from the edition of 18 December 1852 and the two (right) from that of 21 February 1883 (above 150x355; centre right 60x230; below right 65x230).

SOUTH SIDE OF CITY

NORTH SIDE OF CITY

21

Joseph Pennell produced the top sketch for inclusion in Mrs Schuyler Van Rensselaer's *English Cathedrals* of 1887. It was actually drawn in 1885 and was obviously the inspiration for the view below by E. Eldon Deane, which comes from Anna Bowman Dodd's *Cathedral Days*, also of 1887. Both publications are American and Deane in producing his view would therefore have been familiar with Pennell's work. The latter is a summer scene and the former is drawn in winter with no foliage on the trees or luxuriant grass on the river bank (above 50x90; below 85x140).

A distant view of Salisbury from the south-east. It is included in Volume 10 of the *Antiquarian and Topographical Cabinet* published by James Sargant Storer and John Greig between 1807 and 1811. The artist is J. Brokendon and the engraver Storer himself (58x88).

An ethereal glimpse of the Cathedral spire by R.E.J. Bush from Ernest Wall's *Salisbury Avon* of 1929 (85x125).

A sketch of the Cathedral spire through the trees by Joseph Pennell. It comes from the 1905 illustrated edition of Henry James' *English Hours*, originally published in 1875 (90x67).

Two middle distance views of the Cathedral by Joseph Pennell from Mrs Schuyler Van Rensselaer's *English Cathedrals* of 1887. The one (left) is over the roofs of houses in the City and that below from the Bishop's garden (left 175x125; below 100x130).

Two roughly similar views of the Cathedral from the north-west. The one (left) is by Charles E. Flower and comes from E.E. Dorling's *History of Salisbury* of 1911. That below is by Alexander Ansted and is included in *Our English Minsters* of 1893 by F.W. Farrer with the Salisbury section by the then Dean, G.D. Boyle (left 90x75; below 125x75).

Two views in high summer with the Cathedral embowered in trees. That (right) is by Nelly Erichsen from Edward Hutton's *Highways and Byways in Wiltshire* of 1917. The one below is by Joseph Pennell from the 1905 illustrated edition of Henry James' *English Hours*, originally published in 1875 (right 135x90; below 67x90).

CITY CENTRE

The City centre was laid out on a modified grid pattern roughly at the same time as the Cathedral and Close from 1220 onwards and gradually incorporated an existing settlement on the east around St Martin's church. The new urban area was planned on a generous scale and included a large and important market place with the layout of the streets being designed to ensure the proper flow of water in the channels through them. Although the grid pattern was modified, it did produce a number of squares or rectangles, which became known as chequers after the pattern of a chessboard, or more likely the medieval method of keeping accounts on a squared cloth. These chequers were usually named after their most prominent building, often an inn, which rather goes against G.K. Chesterton's light-hearted assertion that the rolling English drunkard made the rolling English road.

Salisbury became a centre of the wool trade and reached the height of its prosperity in the fifteenth century when it was ranked third in importance among the provincial towns of England. There were the usual public buildings and one of the most interesting was an Elizabethan Council House, that went up in flames in 1780 after a particularly splendid night of entertaining and carousing. It was replaced on a nearby site overlooking the Market Place with a Guildhall designed by Sir Robert Taylor and actually constructed by William Pilkington between 1788 and 1795. As a building it has a rather stately air with a facade of six Tuscan columns and much rustication.

The former St Edmund's College was in private hands from the mid-sixteenth century until 1871 when it became a school and in 1927 was acquired by the City and became the present Council House with appropriate office conversion for local authority use. The south front was a mid-eighteenth century conversion rather in the style of James Gibbs.

The Poultry Cross on the edge of the Market Square is a much loved feature of the City and it has been suggested that its name comes from the world poletria meaning horses not fowl. Whatever the explanation, the Cross forms a pleasant termination to the southwest corner of the Market Square, especially as it is surrounded by such appropriate names as Butcher Row, Fish Row, Ox Row and Oatmeal Row. It is worth noting in conclusion that Salisbury has a particularly rich heritage of street names, some of which have changed markedly through time. It is always a fairly safe bet that in most towns New Street usually describes one of the oldest thoroughfares and Salisbury is no exception, as that particular name dates from at least as far back as 1265.

The Poultry Cross as it appeared in the eighteenth century and the first half of the nineteenth century without the present familiar and elegant upper section. James Basire is the engraver of this drawing and it comes from Volume 9 of the Society of Antiquaries' publication *Archaeologia* with a date of 14 May 1789 (105x130).

The Poultry Cross as restored by Owen Browne Carter, a Winchester architect, who designed the Corn Exchange (now public library) in that City with a portico strongly reminiscent of St Paul's, Covent Garden, by Inigo Jones. Carter also produced a set of engravings in 1830 entitled *Picturesque Memorials of Winchester*. This anonymous wood-engraved view of the restored cross comes from the *Illustrated London News* of 26 March 1853, but the statues in the niches were never actually included. Carter's inspiration for the restoration seems to have been the Chichester Cross, as a water colour of it by him forms the frontispiece to Percy D. Mundy's *Memorials of Old Sussex* of 1909 (160x155).

Things are not always quite what they seem. This view of the Poultry Cross is included in Peter Hall's *Picturesque Memorials of Salisbury* of 1834 and would thus appear to pre-date Owen Browne Carter's additions to the upper sections by nearly twenty years. However, the text makes it quite clear that this is merely J. Fisher the artist floating ideas. The wording reads: 'The restorations here proposed are simple and appropriate; would it be thought extravagant to hope that something of the kind might at no distant day be carried into execution?' The figure in the centre leaning against the parapet is an aimiable and eccentric character who was known as 'Alderman' Sutton. He died in 1821 and carried out the highly unlikely joint professions of surgeon and baker, so this view should be treated in its entirety with great circumspection (100x165).

A further view of the Poultry Cross from the *Illustrated London News*. It is dated 31 August 1872 and the artist is Samuel Read (110x95).

The Poultry Cross is shown in an almost empty street with only the woman and presumably her son on the right. It is a sketch by Herbert Railton from W. Outram Tristram's *Coaching Days and Coaching Ways* of 1888. Railton was fond of putting ordinary people in his studies and they were often quite elderly and leaning on sticks (105x85).

Two views of the Poultry Cross by Alfred Rimmer. The one above comes from his *Ancient Stone Crosses of England* of 1875, while that below is from his *Ancient Streets and Homesteads of England* of 1877 and shows a lively market day scene. (above 105x85; below 80x95).

The Market Cross
Salisbury.
Wilts

Fred Roe
Octr 1908

A fascinating study in Edwardian costume near the Poultry Cross. The full-bosomed and long-skirted woman with an umbrella marches imperiously towards the man beside the horse, as another man in farming dress looks as if he has paused to lean on his stick and light a pipe. The artist is Fred Roe and the sketch of 1908 comes from P.H. Ditchfield's *Vanishing England* of 1910 (130x115).

In this view dated 1932 the Poultry Cross appears to be operating largely as a flower market with the fashionable cloche hats of the period in evidence. It comes from R. Grundy Heape's *Salisbury – Some Architecture in the City and the Close* of 1934 (180x130).

Salisbury
The Poultry Cross

This view of the Poultry Cross is the first example in this work of Henry Sheppard Dale's powerful etchings and it is hard to fathom exactly what the two figures in the foreground are doing. St Thomas' church is prominent in the background and there is a great deal of other closely observed architectural detail (300x200).

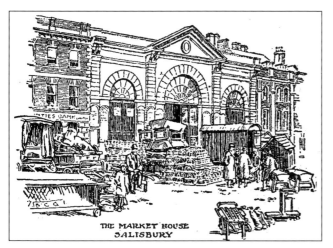 

Two sketches by by Bernard C. Gotch of Salisbury Market, one of the Market House and the other of stalls. They come from W.H. Hudson's *A Shepherd's Life* of 1910 (Market House 65x90; stalls 55x90).

The interior of the Market House. A wood engraving from the *Illustrated London News* of 18 June 1859. There was originally a branch line from the main railway station into the Market House and the latter was designed appropriately by John Strapp, the Chief Engineer of the L.S.W. Railway. The writer of an accompanying article in the *Illustrated London News* likened what was basically a large shed to being 'somewhat after the style of the Crystal Palace'. The rather pleasing facade was kept when the building was converted for use as the public library in 1975, but the shed behind was demolished (170x230).

Three views in and about Salisbury market. Above dealers sizing up cattle, a sketch by Dora Noyes from Ella Noyes *Salisbury Plain* of 1913. Below carriers' carts, a drawing by Bernard C. Gotch from W.H. Hudson's *A Shepherd's Life* of 1910 and right Edmund H. New's representation of a quiet day when the market is closed from Bertram C.A. Windle's *The Wessex of Thomas Hardy* of 1902 (dealers 70x105; carriers' carts 50x90; closed market 145x90).

A busy market day with cattle and horses being inspected. The artist is R.E.J. Bush and the sketch comes from Ernest Wall's *Salisbury Avon* of 1929 (90x90).

Prosperous looking horse dealers and farmers inspect animals offered for sale. A sketch by Bernard C. Gotch from W.H. Hudson's *A Shepherd's Life* of 1910 (45x90).

Three views of the Old George Inn in the High Street. Above a sketch by the architect Maurice Adams on an Architectural Association excursion in August 1876. It comes from the *Building News* of 19 August of the same year (130x170). Below left a view by J. Fisher from Peter Hall's *Picturesque Memorials of Salisbury* of 1834 (105x80). Below right the High Street looking south towards the Cathedral with the Old George on the left. It comes from W. Outram Tristram's *Coaching Days and Coaching Ways* of 1888 and the artist is Herbert Railton (65x90).

Three views of public houses by Herbert Railton from W. Outram Tristram's *Coaching Days and Coaching Ways* of 1888. (Top) the Three Swans in Winchester Street, an eighteenth century building no longer used for its original purpose (75x90). Left the Catherine Wheel partially of the fifteenth century in Milford Street, also no longer serving its original use (95x65). Above the courtyard of what is now the King's Arms Hotel in St John's Street. This is of the late sixteenth century and the first half of the seventeenth with later extensive remodelling, while parts of the building are now in separate occupation (65x90).

The Pheasant Inn in Salt Lane is of late fifteenth-century construction. The artist of this sketch is R.E.J. Bush and it comes from Ernest Wall's *Salisbury Avon* of 1929 (85x85).

Numbers 15-18 Queen Street, dating from the fourteenth to the nineteenth century, and extensively altered in 1970, originally formed the Plume of Feathers Inn. This pencil drawing of the entrance staircase is by R. Grundy Heape and comes from his *Salisbury – Some Architecture in the City and Close* of 1934 (145x115).

Joiners Hall is now owned by the National Trust and was originally built to be a small provincial version of the halls of the City of London livery companies. It was one of a number of similar buildings once in use in Salisbury. Above a view drawn and etched by J. Fisher for Peter Hall's *Picturesque Memorials of Salisbury* of 1834 (175x120). Left a sketch by Charles E. Flower from E.E. Dorling's *History of Salisbury* of 1911 (130x75).

Two door cases in St Ann's Street. Above is number 14 and on the right is number 68. Both are from drawings by R. Grundy Heape in his *Salisbury – Some Architecture in the City and Close* of 1934 (left 80x115; right 115x105).

John Hall was a rich wool merchant and mayor of Salisbury three times in the 1450s and 1460s and parliamentary representative in 1460 and 1461. His house was built on a scale befitting such an important personage and the hall has a splendid open timber roof of six bays restored in 1834 by Augustus Welby Pugin. The facade of the building seen here is of 1881 by the architect Fred Bath. The drawing is by R. Grundy Heape, also from his *Salisbury – Some Architecture in the City and Close* of 1934, by which time the frontage had become the unlikely entrance to the Gaumont cinema (155x100).

The hall of John Hall's house. Left is a view engraved by J. Fisher for Peter Hall's *Picturesque Memorials of Salisbury* of 1834. Most of Fisher's drawings are dated 1832, so presumably the one above pre-dates Pugin's restorations. Hall's text makes it clear that the furniture is imaginary and so also presumably is the quaintly dressed figure, which is probably meant to represent John Hall himself (135x110). Below a sketch of the hall when it had become the entrance hall to the Gaumont cinema. The drawing is by R. Grundy Heape from his *Salisbury – Some Architecture in the City and Close* of 1934 (180x130).

This engraving by John Chessel Buckler comes from his *Sixty Views of Endowed Grammar Schools* of 1827. The Salisbury school is the building behind the railings on the right, which was situated in Castle Street opposite Chipper Lane. It hardly rated as a centre of academic excellence, as from 1804 to 1855 the office of master was held by the same reverend gentleman, who never had more than 22 pupils and hardly ever bothered to turn up to instruct them (95x145).

A view in Castle Street looking south towards the Cathedral. The artist is William Henry Bartlett and the etcher J.C. Varrall. It is dated 1 August 1829 and comes from John Britton's *Picturesque Antiquities of the English Cities*, which appeared originally in six numbers from 1828 to 1830. A great deal of activity is going on in the street with pedestrians, the flock of sheep, women washing clothes in the water courses, people in conversation and a man with a scythe over his shoulder on the left of the donkey with panniers (155x210).

An engraving of Silver Street on what is obviously a busy market day with the Cathedral prominent above the roof tops. An old lady is being helped across one of the small bridges spanning the watercourse near the lampost, while in the foreground a workman is cleaning a long handled instrument of some kind in the same watercourse and presumably making it malodorous in the process. The artist responsible for the street and buildings is William Henry Bartlett, while the figures are drawn by W.H. Brooke. The engraver is John Le Keux and the view dated 1 December 1829 comes from John Britton's *Picturesque Antiquities of the English Cities* (210x155).

A view in the High Street looking south towards the north gate of the Close and the tower, spire and west front of the Cathedral. A horse and cart turn into New Street, a waggon is loaded on the right, an enormous barrel is being manoeuvred on the left and a man climbs a ladder towards an upper floor window. One of the City's watercourses is delineated in the foreground near the woman holding the child's hand with a dog prancing ahead of her. The street and buildings are drawn by William Henry Bartlett and the figures by W.H. Brooke. The engraver of this lively scene dated 1 June 1829 is John Le Keux and it comes from John Britton's *Picturesque Antiquities of the English Cities* (205x155).

This splendid building was the Old Council House, which was destroyed by fire in 1780 'after the annual feast provided for the citizens by the Mayor Elect'. Presumably the wine flowed a little too freely and nobody extinguished all the naked flames before the assembled company staggered off into the night. The building in the background with timber decoration was 'Mr. Wheeler's shop, also destroyed by fire at a later date'. The drawing and engraving is by J. Fisher and comes from Peter Hall's *Picturesque Memorials of Salisbury* of 1834 (100x170).

Trinity Hospital in the street of the same name was founded as an almshouse in 1379 and the present building was constructed in 1702. The chapel was refurnished in 1908 and modernisation in 1950 reduced the accommodation from twelve to ten people. The sketch is by Charles E. Flower from E. E. Dorling's *History of Salisbury* of 1911 (100x70).

There seems to have been a great deal of confusion about the use of the names Church House, the Workhouse and Audley House in Crane Street. The main building is Church House and now used for diocesan purposes. The north range is probably fifteenth century, the west range sixteenth century and the south range eighteenth century. Audley House is also eighteenth century and until the late nineteenth century the eastern most part of the north range of Church House was annexed to Audley House, probably for use as domestic offices. From 1634 to 1881 Church House was the City's workhouse and in 1880 it was offered for sale on condition that it was demolished to allow street widening, a new bridge and another building set farther back. The *Builder* led the objection to this proposed demolition and Church and Audley House were saved with later alterations by Crickmay of Weymouth. The various parts of the building sketched by H.W. Brewer from the *Builder* of 4 June 1881 (left 150x285; two lower sections each 100x165).

Two further views of Church House. Above by Nelly Erichsen from Edward Hutton's *Highways and Byways in Wiltshire* of 1917 (70x90). Below by Herbert Railton from W. Outram Tristram's *Coaching Days and Coaching Ways* of 1888 (125x90).

Two more views of Church House. The one left by J. Fisher in its workhouse days from Peter Hall's *Picturesque Memorials of Salisbury* of 1834 (105x80) and that below by John L. Elyard from his *Old Wiltshire Homes* of 1894 (240x240).

'The Hall', number 4 New Street, is a grand town house now used as offices, which has a certain amount of medieval and seventeenth century work built into its present structure of the mid-eighteenth century. The drawing is by R. Grundy Heape from his *Salisbury – Some Architecture in the City and Close* of 1934 (110x115).

De Vaux College was founded in 1262 by Bishop Bridport to accommodate 20 students from Oxford, who had migrated to Salisbury because of the disturbed times. The building no longer exists, but small parts of it have been incorporated into some of the houses built on the site in De Vaux Place. This view by R. Benson is dated 1820 and comes from Peter Hall's *Picturesque Memorials of Salisbury* of 1834 (100x170).

A view along Crane Street looking towards the then workhouse (now Church House). It is by J. Fisher dated 1832 and comes from Peter Hall's *Picturesque Memorials of Salisbury* of 1834 (115x170).

Numbers 37 the High Street and 79 New Street are adjacent and form one shop. Both are of the early sixteenth century and it is customary for the Bishops of Salisbury to use the premises for robing before their enthronement. It has thus also become customary to call the shop Mitre House and on this view by R. Grundy Heape from his *Salisbury – Some Architecture in the City and Close* a mitre can be seen on the New Street facade immediately below the roof level (150x115).

Two buildings in Harnham depicted in Peter Hall's *Picturesque Memorials of Salisbury* of 1834. That above is St John's Chapel and already described as 'ruinous'. The etcher is C. Castle and J. Fisher is the artist responsible for the view below of Harnham Mill in 1832 (St John's Chapel 100x165; Harnham Mill 115x170).

Harnham Bridge with the Cathedral tower and spire in the distance. The sketch is by Charles E. Flower from E.E. Dorling's *History of Salisbury* of 1911 (60x120).

A view by J. Fisher of the Waggon and Horses public house at Fisherton as it appeared in 1834 in Peter Hall's *Picturesque Memorials of Salisbury* (50x85).

Milford Bridge crosses the road over two distinct channels of the River Bourne on the eastern side of the City and is of late fourteenth or early fifteenth century construction. It seems to have been widened in the eighteenth century. The artist of this drawing is Nelly Erichsen and it comes from Edward Hutton's *Highways and Byways in Wiltshire* in 1917 (60x90).

The wood engraved blackness of this anonymous illustration captures perfectly the misery of flooded homes and businesses at Fisherton in the obviously unrelenting weather. People's possessions are floating away and a lady is being carried over the newly created stream. This engraving comes from the *Illustrated London News* of 11 December 1852 (155x190).

Crane Bridge crosses the River Avon at the western end of Crane Street. It is mostly seventeenth century with the eastern arch possibly partly medieval. The present structure was widened in 1898 and again in 1970. Above a sketch by Herbert Railton from W. Outram Tristram's *Coaching Days and Coaching Ways* of 1888 (65x90). Below a drawing by Fred Roe from P.H. Ditchfield's *Vanishing England* of 1910 (160x115).

THE CATHEDRAL

Rome wasn't built in a day and nor was Salisbury, but of all the English cathedrals it comes closest to being all of a piece rather than an amalgam of widely differing architectural periods. It was also built at quite astonishing speed, as from the laying of the foundation stones in 1220 to the completion of the main fabric, including the detached bell tower and heightened main tower and spire, only a little over a century elapsed. The Hungerford and Beauchamp chapels north and south of the Lady chapel came in the fifteenth century, but with the detached bell tower were swept away by James Wyatt at the end of the eighteenth century. It thus remains the most perfect example of the Early English style in the country and the builders obviously took advantage of working on a completely new and open site. The architect responsible for this magnificent construction is not known exactly, but the most likely candidate appears to be Elias de Dereham. He was a Canon of Salisbury, had many friends in high places and was an extremely able churchman and administrator. In addition, he was intimately involved in the world of art and architecture.

The plan of the building is very regular. The Lady chapel projects two bays and the retrochoir also has two bays with the main choir having seven bays. The small east transepts are two bays, the main transepts three bays and the nave ten bays. There is also a handsome north porch and for a non-monastic foundation a most sumptuous cloister, with a chapter house connected to it by a two bay corridor. The western facade had its statuary almost entirely renewed by Redfern in 1862 and must be accounted one of the least successful parts of the edifice.

The Cathedral originally only had a low lantern tower covering the crossing and the survival of the heightened tower and spire, constructed in the 1330s, is something of a miracle, not least because the great extra weight did not cause the collapse of that part of the building. The interior bracing of the strainer and scissor arches bear eloquent witness to the need for added support to what was a daring and risky concept. However, the result has been a most beautiful tower and slender spire with exquisite ball-flower decoration rising to 404 feet, the highest in England. It is the one feature above all others that seems to symbolise the whole Cathedral, especially of course when seen from a distance.

Time and weather combine to create maintenance problems for any building and in addition tastes change and alterations are made. Francis Price was surveyor to the Cathedral in the mid-eighteenth century and proved to be highly competent and sensible. This contribution to the maintenance of the fabric seems to have been undervalued, not least because it has been overshadowed by James Wyatt's activities towards the end of the same century. Wyatt was aided and abetted by Bishop Shute Barrington in his work of renovation and restoration and the result was met with outrage and condemnation at the time. As one of the most fashionable architects of the period, Wyatt suffered from being lionised, took on too many commissions and left too much to subordinates. John Britton in his *Cathedral Antiquities* gives a full account of Wyatt's activities and points out that some of the criticism was misplaced. By Wyatt's day the Hungerford and Beauchamp chapels had been neglected to the point where they had become decayed and the haunt of spiders and also repositories of unwanted lumber. They were removed and at the same time the renewal and restoration of other parts of the fabric was undertaken.

Sir George Gilbert Scott carried out another programme of renewal and restoration in the 1860s and in turn swept away a good deal of Wyatt's work. It is ironic that his own iron screen and reredos of 1863 lasted barely a century and were removed in 1960. Wyatt had tidied up the tombs and monuments inside the Cathedral in an orderliness, which was almost military in its precision. This is especially true in the nave where they are arranged in a line on the sleeper walls between the arcade piers. The majority of the remaining tombs and monuments scattered throughout the building are interesting rather than outstanding and Salisbury cannot match the rich group of chantries in its near neighbour Winchester. However, the monument to Sir Thomas Gorges and the Audley chantry in the retrochoir, the outstanding monument to Giles de Bridport between the chancel aisle and the east aisle of the south eastern transept, the enormous brass to Bishop Wyville in the north eastern transept and Bishop Mitford's tomb chest in the western part of the south choir aisle are all worthy of the most careful scrutiny.

The interior of the Cathedral has a certain coolness, even perhaps coldness arising from the extensive use of both polished and unpolished Purbeck marble in the piers and shafts, which has given rise to the rather silly jibe about their resemblance to drain pipes. Unlike a cathedral such as Beauvais with its immense height, Salisbury has relatively low vaults and also a gallery, so these piers and shafts help to emphasise the vertical in a building where the horizontal would be otherwise dominant. In conclusion it must be said that the exterior uncluttered view with the Cathedral standing amid its lawns and trees is superb and bids fair to be one of the finest pieces of siting in the whole country.

The detached bell tower with stood to the north of the Cathedral was removed by Wyatt when carrying out his restoration at the end of the eighteenth century. This rather crude anonymous drawing from the *Gentleman's Magazine* of October 1819 shows how much it was missed some thirty years after its disappearance (165x75).

The original spire on the bell tower gave cause for concern in the mid-eighteenth century and Francis Price, surveyor to the Cathedral, produced this plan for its restoration in his *A Series of Observations on the Cathedral Church of Salisbury* of 1753. The engraver of the plan is P. Fourdrinier (205x145).

Two views featuring the detached bell tower. The one above published as late as 1843 by J.H. Nichols was based on a drawing by John Buckler and shows the simple capping that replaced its spire in 1768, fifty years before the view from the *Gentleman's Magazine* on the previous page. Francis Price's scheme, also shown on the previous page, was obviously rejected for something more modest and no doubt cheaper (190x250). The view below is an engraving by E. Easton of 1761 and shows the bell tower with its spire in place (180x280).

A north view of the Cathedral, which appeared originally in Sir William Dugdale's *Monasticon Anglicanum* published between 1655 and 1673. The engravings for this work are almost all by Daniel King from a number of artists including Wenceslas Hollar and were later used by King for his 1656 publication *The Cathedrall and Conventuall Churches of England and Wales*. However, this particular rather crude engraving is anonymous and the artist has made the spire much dumpier and less elegant than in reality (200x310).

A view of the Cathedral from the north in Volume 1 of H. and B. Winkles' *Cathedral Churches of England and Wales* of 1836 to 1842. The Winkles family had connections with a firm of steel engravers in Karlsruhe as early as 1824 and this new process allowed many more reproductions to be made than on the much softer copper plates generally in use until the 1820s. The text of the work is by Thomas Moule, whose fame rests much more on his cartographic endeavours. The artist is Hablot Browne and the engraver Henry Winkles himself. Hablot Browne was apprenticed to the well-known Finden brothers, Edward and William, and went on to become one of the best illustrators of Dickens' novels with the nickname 'Phiz'. Even at this early stage of his career his lively interest in people is evident from the number included in this view, which Henry Winkles interprets with great sensitivity, especially the stormy skies and flocks of birds round the spire (140x115).

This is the first of a number of copper engravings in the present work taken from John Britton's *Cathedral Antiquities* and is dated 2 June 1815. It is a view of the north porch of the Cathedral engraved by John Le Keux from a drawing by Frederick Mackenzie. The three promenading people make an opulent comparison with the simply attired figure sitting in the porch, while the couple on the extreme right are admiring the main fabric of the building (205x155).

An engraving of the north porch of the Cathedral from the *Builder* of 28 July 1849.
The artist is W. Caveler and the engraver somebody simply called Laing (225x165).

A cloudy summer's day with shafts of light casting deep shadows on the facade of the Cathedral in this north eastern view dated 1 January 1815 from John Britton's *Cathedral Antiquities*. The artist is Frederick Mackenzie and the engraver Henry Le Keux, the brother of John Le Keux. The tiny figures beside one of the buttresses near the centre of the facade and under the trees on the right emphasise the great size of the building, the representation of which is highly detailed even down to the lightning conductor on the spire (150x200).

Frederick Nash was employed for the Society of Antiquaries volumes of *Vetusta Monumenta* covering the Tower of London in 1815 and the Temple Church in 1818. He had worked previously for Storer and Greig's *Select Views of London and Its Environs* of 1804 and this close up of the north porch of the Cathedral is the first of his drawings in the present book from William Dodsworth's *Historical Account of the Episcopal See and Cathedral Church* of Salisbury of 1814. The engraver is John Hawksworth, who was also employed to produce plates for Britton and Pugin's *Public Buildings of London* of 1825-1828 and Brayley and Britton's *Westminster Palace* of 1836 (230x190).

F. Price Delin 1747.

P. Fourdrinier Sculp.ᵗ

A plan and north-east perspective of the Cathedral in 1747 before Wyatt's alterations. It comes from Francis Price's *A Series of Observations on the Cathedral Church of Salisbury* of 1753. The artist is Price himself and the engraver P. Fourdrinier, who also produced two plates for the sixth edition of Stow's *Survey of London* in 1754 (235x255).

Frederick Nash is the artist for this north-eastern view of the Cathedral from William Dodsworth's *Historical Account of the Episcopal See and Cathedral Church of Salisbury* of 1814, which is also the date of the engraving itself. The size and majesty of the Cathedral are emphasised by the two small figures in white standing against the facade and deep shadows are cast by the sun on this cloudy day in high summer. The engraver is William Woolnoth, who worked with Nash on Brayley and Britton's *Westminster Palace* of 1836 and also contributed widely to the massive series of volumes in the *Beauties of England and Wales* from 1810 to 1816 (225x185).

Another cloudy day in high summer throwing long shadows in this wood engraved north-eastern view of the Cathedral. It comes from Richard John King's *Handbook to the Cathedrals of England* published by John Murray in 1861. The artist and engraver is Orlando Jewitt (130x105).

A north-eastern view of the Cathedral. It is a wood engraving by H.E. Sylvester from a drawing of 1885 by Joseph Pennell depicting a summer's day and comes from Mrs Schuyler Van Rensselaer's *English Cathedrals* of 1887 (125x170).

A highly sophisticated piece of engraving by John Le Keux dated 1 February 1815, which has subtle and delicate variations in the lighting to emphasise differing architectural features of the Cathedral's east end. Shafts of light shine through the clouds on this summer's day and between buttresses on the left a man points out a feature with a stick to his wife. A child appears to be sitting in a pram next to him, while a number of people are walking about under the trees on the extreme right. The artist is Frederick Mackenzie and the engraving comes from John Britton's *Cathedral Antiquities* (200x150).

Above is a south-eastern view of the Cathedral by John Chessel Buckler from his *Views of Cathedral Churches of England and Wales* of 1822 (180x255). Below the Cathedral also seen from the south-east by Thomas Hearne from his *Antiquities of Great Britain*, which was issued in parts from 1777-1786, most of the engravings including this one being by William Byrne. The date is 31 March 1798 and, although nearly a decade after Wyatt's alterations to the building, still shows the Beauchamp chapel on the left and the Hungerford chapel on the right (185x255).

The Reverend John Louis Petit was of Huguenot descent and this sketch of
the Cathedral from the south-east comes from his *Remarks on Architectural
Character* of 1846 (315x240).

A view by Nelly Erichsen entitled the *Cathedral from the Palace Garden*. It comes from *Highways and Byways in Wiltshire* by Edward Hutton of 1917 (130x90).

A summer storm is brewing in this south-eastern view of the Cathedral and birds fly round the spire. An ecclesiastic talks to a friend, while visitors inspect the building in the background. The artist is John Wykeham Archer, a native of Newcastle, who with Hablot Browne trained under the engravers Edward and William Finden. Archer was responsible for steel and wood engraved plates in a number of publications and this view comes Volume 1 of H. and B. Winkles' *Cathedral Churches of England and Wales* published from 1836 to 1842. The engraver is Henry Winkles himself (140x110).

The storm appears about to burst upon the people and dog running to take shelter in this anonymous wood engraved south-easterly view of the Cathedral. It comes from the April 1881 edition of *Harpers*, the American monthly magazine (165x110).

Arthur Wilde Parsons is the artist of this study of the Cathedral from the Bishop's garden. It comes from the *Cathedrals of England and Wales* by Charles Whibley of 1888, which was printed in Nuremberg (230x175).

A southern view of the Cathedral from the Bishop's garden dated 1813, which depicts an atmospheric, cloudy day in summer with the chapter house in sunlight against the surrounding darkness of foliage and trees. The artist is Frederick Mackenzie and the engraver Samuel Mitan and the view comes from William Dodsworth's *Historical Account of the Episcopal See and Cathedral Church of Salisbury* of 1814. Mitan engraved a few plates for Rudolph Ackermann, but was not used widely for topographical work (210x150).

The Cathedral from the Bishop's garden in 1887.
One of Henry Sheppard Dale's powerful etchings
(300x200).

A view of the east end of the Cathedral from volume two of John Britton's *Beauties of Wiltshire* of 1801. The artist is Britton himself and the engraver James Sargant Storer (135x95).

A south-west view of the Cathedral by Frederick Nash from William Dodsworth's *Historical Account of the Episcopal See and Cathedral Church of Salisbury* of 1814. The engraver is George Cooke, who was apprenticed to James Basire senior and cut his teeth on work for the *Beauties of England and Wales*. George collaborated with other members of his family in producing topographical work and his favourite publication was his *Views in London and Its Vicinity* issued in parts between 1826 and 1834 (125x165).

One of Henry Sheppard Dale's etchings of the Cathedral, this time from Harnham meadows (300x200).

The west front of the Cathedral. A finely detailed drawing by Francis Price dated 1738 from his work *A Series of Observations on the Cathedral Church of Salisbury* of 1753. The engraver is P. Fourdrinier (205x145).

The west front of the Cathedral drawn by Frederick Mackenzie and engraved by John Le Keux. Parts of the facade are lit by sunlight on a cloudy summer day and a small procession is emerging through the west door. The engraving comes from John Britton's *Cathedral Antiquities* and is dated 1 August 1814 (205x155).

A view of the west front of the Cathedral dated 1813 and engraved by Samuel Mitan from a drawing by Frederick Nash. An isolated ecclesiastical figure in black on the right gives scale to the building, as also do the woman and child on the extreme left. The work comes from William Dodsworth's *Historical Account of the Episcopal See and Cathedral Church of Salisbury* of 1814 (215x160).

John Britton is the artist for this view of the west front of the Cathedral, which forms the frontispiece of Volume 1 of his *Beauties of Wiltshire*, his native county. The date of the work is 1801 and the engraver of the view James Sargant Storer (155x100).

James Sargant Storer is also the engraver for this view of the west front of the Cathedral from a drawing by his son Henry. It comes from Volume 4 of James Sargant Storer's *History and Antiquities of the Cathedral Churches of Great Britain* of 1819 (115x80).

One of Hablot Browne's detailed drawings of the Cathedral showing an ecclesiastical procession and groups of visitors outside the west front. It comes from volume 1 of H. and B. Winkles' *Cathedral Churches of England and Wales* of 1836-1842. The engraver is Henry Winkles himself and even though the scene is obviously in high summer, he has not resisted the temptation to add a stormy sky with shafts of sunlight creating an interesting pattern of shadows on the facade (145x110).

The west front was restored by Sir George Gilbert Scott in the early 1860s and Redfern was responsible for the renovation and replacement of some 60 statues. This anonymous wood engraving comes from volume 1 of *Our National Cathedrals* of 1887 (145x100).

William Henry James Boot was art editor of the *Strand* from 1895 to 1915 and provided a large number of drawings for illustrations in late Victorian and Edwardian periodicals and books. This detailed wood engraving appeared in several books including *Picturesque Europe* and the *Rivers of Britain*. The carter allowing the horse to drink its fill makes a pleasing everyday contrast with the majesty of the Cathedral seen from the north-west. This particular version of the engraving comes from T.G. Bonney's *Cathedrals, Abbeys and Churches of England and Wales* of 1891 (225x150).

Salisbury Cathedral
The Western Doorways

Plate II

1887

The western doorways of the Cathedral are shown at an unusual angle in this etching by Henry Sheppard Dale of 1887. Human interest has been added by the mysterious figure emerging from the shadows of the trees, presumably for a pre-arranged assignation with the woman standing by the buttress (300x200).

A highly detailed and lively depiction of the western doorways of the Cathedral by A.B. Pite. It comes from the *Builder* of 26 January 1884 (280x190).

A north-western view of the Cathedral by John Chessel Buckler from his *Views of Cathedral Churches in England and Wales* of 1822. It is a smaller version of his father, John Buckler's, work of 1803 and shows how talent can pass down the generations (180x255).

The Cathedral seen from the North Canonry garden in the Close. A sketch by R. Grundy Heape from his *Salisbury – Some Architecture in the City and Close* of 1934 (180x135).

The Cathedral seen from the north-west by William Weihe Collins on a balmy summer's day with towering trees covered in foliage prominent around the building. It comes from *Cathedral Cities of England* of 1905 by George Gilbert (100x150).

A curious invitation card drawn and engraved by Thomas Burrough in 1734 showing the Cathedral from the south-west with a dream-like foreground. It does however show the library built over the east range of the cloisters in the mid-fifteenth century, that was partially demolished in 1758 (205x115).

Sr

Briſtol

You are desired to meet your Countrymen, Gentlemen Natives of the County of **Wilts**, at the Tolzey on   to accom=
=pany the Preſident to   Church, to
hear a Sermon, from thence to the
      to Dinner, bringing this Ticket with you.

Preſident

Tho: Burrough delin. et Sculp.ʳ *1734*:

A view of the Cathedral from the cloisters almost identical with a drawing by Turner in the Victoria and Albert Museum. It is dated 1 August 1814 and comes from John Britton's *Cathedral Antiquities*. The artist is Frederick Mackenzie and the engraver John Le Keux (210x150).

Salisbury Cathedral
The Cloisters showing the Library
the Chapter House & the Transepts

One of Henry Sheppard Dale's etchings of 1887 showing parts of the Cathedral and cloisters. What are the two well-dressed ladies actually doing? They must surely be examining some interesting object on the ground, although it is hard to dismiss entirely the unworthy thought that they are spreading a picnic, as the lady standing on the left looks as if she might be holding a bottle of wine in a wicker basket rather than just a rather elaborate handbag (300x200).

A very similar view to that on the previous page. It is by H. H. Statham and comes from the *Builder* of 4 July 1891. The diminutive man with a stick and his hat in hand gazing up at the spire gives some indication of the height and majesty of the whole building (380x280).

Two women and a child stand on the grass in the middle of the cloisters in this view from volume 4 of James Sargant Storer's *History and Antiquities of the Cathedral Churches of Great Britain* of 1819. The engraver is Storer himself from a drawing by his son Henry Sargant and the exact date of the engraving is given as 1 October 1814 (75x115).

Shafts of sunlight penetrate the gloom of the cloisters where a workman seems to be engaged in the unenviable task of clearing a drain. An idler sits on the coping contemplating the scene while a visitor makes an observation to his wife by pointing his stick. The artist is Richard Cattermole and the engraver J. Lewis, about whom very little seems to be known, except that he appears to have been very competent and is recorded as having produced two plates for Edward Wedlake Brayley's *Westminster Abbey*. The engraving is dated 1 April 1815 and comes from John Britton's *Cathedral Antiquities* (155x205).

A measured drawing of three bays of the cloisters. It
is by George O. Scorer and comes from the *Builder* of
31 July 1897 (240x380).

91

Samuel Read is the artist of this atmospheric engraving of the cloisters. From 1844 to 1883 he worked extensively for the *Illustrated London News* both abroad and recording architectural scenes in Britain. It was said that his drawings of castles, cathedrals and ruins were delightfully dank and gloomy with thick undergrowth, that gave the appearance of having been sketched with the aid of melted candlewax. This view is from the *Illustrated London News* of 31 August 1872 (120x180).

A striking etching by C. Castle showing parts of the Cathedral, cloisters, chapter house and the countryside beyond. It comes from Peter Hall's *Picturesque Memorials of Salisbury* of 1834 (195x145).

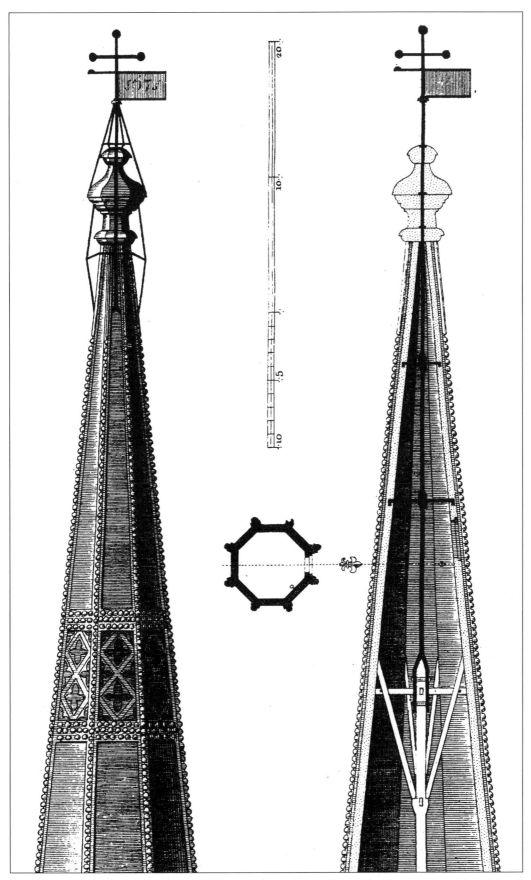

Exterior and interior detailing of the top of the Cathedral spire by Francis Price dated 1746 and published in 1753 in his *A Series of Observations on the Cathedral Church of Salisbury*. The engraver is P. Fourdrinier (200x145).

A powerful engraving from John Britton's *Cathedral Antiquities* detailing part of the tower and spire of the Cathedral. The depiction of the exquisite ball flower decoration is particularly striking. The engraver is John Le Keux from a drawing by Frederick Mackenzie and the date is 1 August 1813 (210x160).

A view of the nave looking east down its length. The etcher is John Le Keux from a drawing by Frederick Mackenzie. The work is dated 1 August 1815 and it comes from John Britton's *Cathedral Antiquities* (200x150).

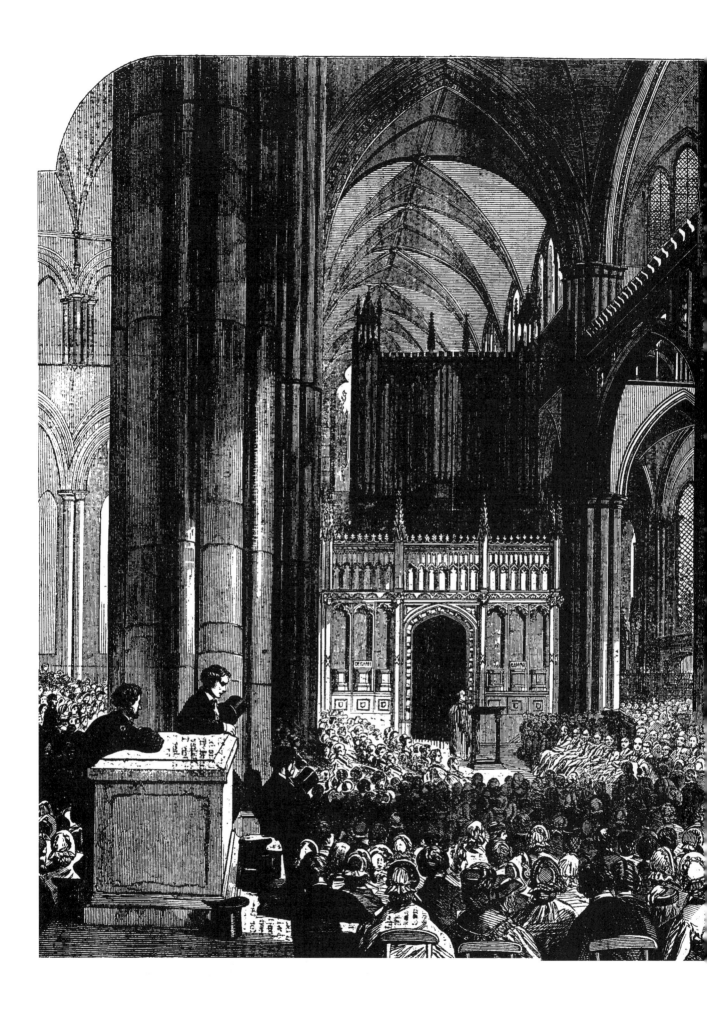

A choir festival in the
Cathedral in the summer
of 1861. An anonymous
wood engraving in the
Illustrated London News of
15 June 1861 (240x345).

The nave of the Cathedral looking west. A view drawn and engraved by Orlando Jewitt for Richard John King's *Handbook to the Cathedrals of England* of 1861 (135x95).

The nave looking east as it was in 1754, a view that was originally drawn by J. Biddlecomb, but this reworking by J. Fisher was etched for Peter Hall's *Picturesque Memorials of Salisbury* of 1834 (165x140).

Within the etching:
Salisbury Cathedral
Tomb of William Longsword
Earl of Salisbury Plate

One of Henry Sheppard Dale's etchings showing the tomb of William Longespée or Longsword, Earl of Salisbury, in the nave of the Cathedral (300x200).

Choristers singing in the choir of the Cathedral during a service with a woman and child listening. The artist is Frederick Nash and the engraver Joseph Skelton. The view comes from William Dodsworth's *Historical Account of the Episcopal See and Cathedral Church of Salisbury* of 1814, which is also the date of this particular engraving (215x180).

Two ecclesiastics being led by a verger beside the Audley chantry with choristers in the background on the left. This view of the Cathedral choir from the Lady chapel is an engraving by George Cooke from a drawing by Frederick Nash and also comes from William Dodsworth's *Historical Account of the Episcopal See and Cathedral Church of Salisbury* of 1814. The engraving itself is dated 1815 and is a good example of how illustrations were often sold separately and incorporated in copies of books bound up and sold later than the original publication date (215x185).

The east end of the choir with the Audley chantry. An engraving by John Le Keux from a drawing by George Cattermole dated 1 November 1820. It comes from John Britton's *Chronological History of English Architecture* (215x155).

A view of the north aisle looking west with the Audley chantry given prominence in the centre of this engraving dated 1 June 1815. The artist is Frederick Mackenzie and the engraver John Le Keux and the view comes from John Britton's *Cathedral Antiquities* (210x155).

The beautiful Purbeck marble and stone monument to Bishop Giles de Bridport, who died in 1262. It is situated between the chancel aisle and the eastern aisle of the south-east transept and has inspired a number of artists to reproduce its complicated detailing. The artist of this view is Frederick Mackenzie and the engraver J. Hobson. The date is 1 August 1815 and the engraving comes from John Britton's *Cathedral Antiquities* (205x160).

Henry Sheppard Dale's etched version of the monument to Bishop Giles de Bridport dated 1887 (300x200).

A detailed drawing of part of Bishop Giles de Bridport's monument by Sir George Gilbert Scot from his *Essay on the History of English Church Architecture* of 1881 (225x150).

A vigorous sketch of part of Bishop Bridport's monument by J. Gibbons Sankey of September 1882. It comes from volume 4 of the New Series of the *Architectural Association's Sketch Books* (300x250).

One of Henry Sheppard Dale's etchings of 1887 showing the south aisle of the choir (300x200).

The artist of this view of the Lady chapel
looking north-east is Richard Cattermole and
the engraver S. Noble. It is dated 2 October
1815 and comes from John Britton's *Cathedral
Antiquities* (205x160).

This view from the north to south transept by Frederick Mackenzie
comes from John Britton's *Cathedral Antiquities*. The engraver is
Henry Le Keux and the date 1 April 1814 (200x145).

A view in the transepts engraved by William Woolnoth from a drawing by Frederick Nash dated 1813. It comes from William Dodsworth's *Historical Account of the Episcopal See and Cathedral Church of Salisbury* of 1814. The two figures in black are either engaged in deep conversation or merely gossiping about this and that (215x180).

A view of the south transept of the Cathedral looking north-west. There is a very subtle play of light in this engraving by John Le Keux from a drawing by Frederick Mackenzie. It is dated 1 August 1814 and comes from John Britton's *Cathedral Antiquities*. One of the strainer arches shows how necessary this added strengthening of the fabric is for the survival of the tower and spire (205x150).

The small transept looking south with the strengthening scissor arches on the right. An engraving by William Smith dated 1 July 1815 from a drawing by Frederick Mackenzie. It comes from John Britton's *Cathedral Antiquities* (205x150).

An outline drawing with a high viewpoint showing a view from the north to south small transept with one of the scissor arches. It is engraved by E. Turrell from a drawing by Frederick Mackenzie dated 1 December 1819 and comes from John Britton's *Chronological History of English Architecture* (210x155).

A view inside the chapter house of the Cathedral emphasing the slenderness of the central column and looking towards the entrance. The engraver is John Le Keux after a drawing by Frederick Mackenzie and the lighting is particularly subtle. The date of the engraving is 1 May 1814 and it comes from John Britton's *Cathedral Antiquities* (195x155).

An almost similar view to the one on the previous page. Well-dressed visitors are being instructed by a guide and shadows creep across the floor. The artist is Frederick Nash with the etching being shared between William Smith and John Pye. It comes from William Dodsworth's *Historical Account of the Episcopal See and Cathedral Church of Salisbury* of 1814 (215x185).

Looking into the chapter house from the area of the entrance with two ecclesiastics in conversation by the table. The view is etched by John Le Keux from a drawing by Richard Cattermole and is dated 1 March 1820. It comes from John Britton's *Chronological History of English Architecture* (210x160).

A man and woman are having a detail on the doorway of the chapter house
pointed out by a verger with shafts of sunlight casting shadows between them.
This view is one of Henry Sheppard Dale's 1887 etchings (300x200).

The chapter house was restored by Henry Clutton, William Burges and George Gilbert Scott by public subscription between 1855 and 1861. This view of 1 November 1856 from the *Illustrated London News* shows well dressed ladies and gentlemen gathered round the central pillar, possibly viewing the work in progress (230x150).

Numbers 1, 3 and 4 are details from the chapter house and 2 is a roof boss in the cloisters in the compartment nearest the chapter house. They were all drawn by Frederick Mackenzie from sketches by T. Baxter and engraved by John Le Keux. The date is 1 March 1814 and the details all come from John Britton's *Cathedral Antiquities* (225x160).

The reredos was designed by Sir George Gilbert Scott in 1873 and is seen in place in this wood engraved view from the *Builder* of 10 March 1877. It was however removed in 1960 (265x170).

Left is a view of Sir George Gilbert Scott's screen and reredos and below the reredos alone. Both screen and reredos were removed in 1960, much to the displeasure of enthusiasts for Victorian architecture. Both illustrations come from *Our National Cathedrals* of 1887 (left 125x100; below 150x100).

Above left the Hungerford chantry and above right the Beauchamp chantry. They were swept away by James Wyatt at the end of the eighteenth century. Originally in Gough's *Sepulchral Monuments* these versions come from Peter Hall's *Picturesque Memorials of Salisbury* of 1834 (each 75x105). Below, what was originally the Cathedral muniment room about which Peter Hall wrote 'Many an antiquary would give his ears for a few weeks' forage among the parchments, which lie at present in most irregular repose – a feast for moths and spiders'. Since 1834 the moths and spiders have been banished and the room has become the treasury (120x160).

THE CLOSE

In continental Europe all life flows up and around the great cathedrals. Markets are held against their steps and walls, loungers drink aperitifs at café tables in their shadow and during daylight hours all is bustle and animation, colour and activity. This is also true of the two great ecclesiastical buildings of London, Westminster Abbey and St Paul's Cathedral. Westminster Abbey indeed has a close, but it in no way impedes the feeling of the endless swirl of traffic, the pomp of great state occasions and the sense of long centuries of worship at the heart of government. In a different but no less tangible way, St Paul's Cathedral symbolises the City of London. Nobody can forget the photograph of its dome standing out against the fires of the Blitz and yet like its continental cousins, it has the immediacy of the everyday. Office workers and young backpackers from abroad munch their sandwiches on its steps, people on the tops of buses pass within what seems to be almost touching distance and in the view up the Thames from Waterloo Bridge, it still stands out as something apart and wonderful against the high rise buildings that crowd round it.

However most English cathedrals are surrounded by a close and nowhere more so than at Salisbury, which has one of the largest and most spacious in the whole country. Indeed the close in Salisbury could well be described as a city within a city, with its own walls and gates and feeling of something quite different from the urban life to its immediate north and east. Even in the early twentieth century, Edward Hutton in his *Highways and Byways in Wiltshire* recalls encountering a man from the local countryside, who asked him somewhat hesitantly if it were permitted actually to enter the Cathedral at the heart of this place so remote from

his everyday experience. Coventry Patmore in one of his poems recalls a visit to the Deanery with the words:

Red brick and ashlar long and low,
With dormers and with oriels lit.
Geraniums, lychnis, rose-arrayed
The windows all wide open thrown;
And someone in the study played
The wedding march of Mendelssohn

This seems a perfect evocation of the nineteenth-century world of Trollopian Barchester and you can almost hear the tinkle of tea-cups and see plates of delicate cucumber sandwiches with their crusts removed.

The construction of the start of the Close precedes even that of the Cathedral itself and the Bishop's Palace appears to have been in existence by 1218, ahead of a wooden chapel the next year and the laying of the foundation stones for the new Cathedral in 1220. The size of the Close seems to have been a very shrewd piece of financial management, as in order to raise funds for the new Cathedral, Bishop Richard Poore managed to persuade many of the clergy and nobility to sign seven year covenants or give outright donations for this massive building project. In return, each of the canons was allowed a 'proper space' for the erection of a dwelling house and this seems to have been interpreted very liberally on what up to then had been an unoccupied area.

Through the centuries most of the houses in the Close have been altered or modified to suit different occupants and uses. There has also been significant and educational involvement in the buildings, which were originally constructed for the use of the clergy. Even today there is still a feeling of a world apart when entry is made through a Close gate and it is somewhat ironic, that the spacious air of repose owes its origins not to piety, but the urgent need to raise cash.

An anonymous view through the military looking Harnham gate into the Close from the south-east. This gate has a platform above a deep arch and the drawing comes from Peter Hall's *Picturesque Memorials of Salisbury* of 1834 (75x55).

The north side of the north gate into the Close on a busy day in the 1830s with well-dressed citizens going about their business. This is the principal gate into the Close. It is partly fourteenth and fifteenth century in origin with later restorations and bears the Stuart royal arms. The porter's lodge is the building on the left just through the arch with the two plants in tubs above the door case, while the gate posts of the College of Matrons can be seen a little farther down the street. The bootmaker, E. Fricker, adds a note of metropolitan tone by proclaiming his origins in New Street; Covent Garden (now New Row an alley between St Martin's Lane and King Street), while the top of the Cathedral spire can be seen above the rooftops. The artist of this view is J. Fisher and it comes from Peter Hall's *Picturesque Memorials of Salisbury* of 1834 (160x110).

This drawing is by Alfred Rimmer from his *Ancient Streets and Homesteads of England* of 1877 and also shows the north side of the north gate into the Close. The bootmaker is now called Newman and the two shoppers on the right are conversing with the easy air of old friends (100x75).

Joseph Pennell's sketch of the north side of the north gate into the Close from Mrs. Schuyler Van Rensselaer's *English Cathedrals* of 1887. The bootmaker's shop on the left has now been taken over by the Singer Sewing Machine Company and on this sleepy day there is nobody visible but one small figure in the Close itself (120x110).

A. Wilson is the artist of this view through the north side of the north gate into the Close and it comes from Charles Whibley's *Cathedrals of England and Wales* of 1888, which was printed in Nuremberg. The College of Matrons can be glimpsed on the left and one of the pinnacles of the Cathedral's west front closes the vista (100x100).

Close of Sarum, Salisbury.

NELLY ERICHSEN.

This highly detailed sketch of the north side of the north gate into the Close is by Nelly Erichsen and comes from Edward Hutton's *Highways and Byways in Wiltshire* of 1917. The bicycle has long since become a favourite form of transport and the Singer Sewing Machine Company is still on the left next to the gate (135x85).

A beautifully detailed etching of the south side of the north gate into the Close by Henry Sheppard Dale. It is dated 1887 and looks northwards into the High Street with the statue in the central niche that of a Stuart monarch. This latter was replaced in 1902 by one of a rotund and prosperous-looking Edward VII in coronation robes. However, at the original date set for the event he fell ill and it had to be postponed for some three months. As the statue was already in place and had been dedicated by the Mayoress at the first date, everybody must have breathed a sigh of relief at his recovery, because you could hardly have left a monarch in that position wearing coronation regalia, if he had died before being crowned (300x200).

The south side of the north gate into the Close shown in this wood engraved view by Samuel Read from the *Illustrated London News* of 31 August 1872. The statue is still that of a Stuart monarch in the central niche (95x100).

One of Nelly Erichsen's sketches from Edward Hutton's *Highways and Byways in Wiltshire* of 1917, which shows the south side of the north gate into the Close. By that date the figure of a Stuart monarch had been replaced in the central niche by the cheerful and well-nourished face of Edward VII in his coronation robes (110x90).

The artist of this powerful etching of the south side of the north gate into the Close is John Moulding Clarke and it comes from the *Builder* of 10 April 1931 (205x140).

St Anne's gate stands at the north-east of the Close and joins North Walk to St Ann's Street. Above is a north-east view from near the King's Arms in St John Street by Herbert Railton and it comes from W. Outram Tristram's *Coaching Days and Coaching Ways* of 1888 (55x90). Below a sketch by Joseph Pennell, which comes from Mrs Schuyler Van Rensselaer's *English Cathedrals* of 1887 (60x95).

An east view of St Ann's gate from Exeter Street by Samuel Read in the *Illustrated London News* of 31 August 1872. This pleasant wood engraving shows two figures chatting on the left and a matronly figure on the right with her shopping baskets. In addition a woman and child can just be glimpsed passing under the arch. However, Read seems to have wasted little time depicting the spire of the Cathedral, which looks as if it were done with the aid of a handy ruler (100x110).

Alfred Rimmer's version of an east view of St Ann's gate from his *Ancient Streets and Homesteads of England* of 1877. There is a great deal going on with the horse and cart, friends in discussion on the left, a woman and child under the arch, a lighting column in the right foreground and a detailed depiction of the tower and spire of the Cathedral (100x75).

A south-east view of St Ann's gate by J. Fisher from Peter Hall's *Picturesque Memorials of Salisbury* of 1834. A well-dressed family stands in the arch of the gate, a barrow with baskets of what appear to be vegetables is being pushed on the left, a lounger leans on a rail, a housewife is burdened with shopping baskets and the scene is completed with two figures in conversation on the right (120x165).

A drawing of St Ann's gate from the south-east by the architect W. Curtis Green. It comes from the *Builder* of 5 August 1899, for which Curtis Green worked for a number of years. During this time he produced beautifully detailed drawings of a wide range of buildings at home and abroad (100x130).

A south-east view of St Ann's gate from Anna Bowman Dodd's *Cathedral Days* of 1887. The artist of the sketch is E. Eldon Deane (80x115).

A drawing by Nelly Erichsen showing an east view of St Ann's gate from the entrance to St Ann's Street. It comes from Edward Hutton's *Highways and Byways in Wiltshire* of 1917 and judging by the shadows the time seems to be about midday (115x90).

In 1947 the former Bishop's Palace became the Cathedral School and the Bishop's residence is now the South Canonry. This north-west view of the Palace by Frederick Nash was engraved by Elizabeth Byrne for William Dodsworth's *Historical Account of the Episcopal See and Cathedral Church of Salisbury* of 1814. Elizabeth Byrne was one of the very few women engravers of the period and sister to William Byrne, who worked with Thomas Hearne on the *Antiquities of Great Britain*, issued in parts from 1777 to 1786 (105x145).

A very similar view to that above showing modifications to the tower on the left. The artist is J. Fisher and the engraving comes from Peter Hall's *Picturesque Memorials of Salisbury* of 1834 (105x170).

Two further views of the former Bishop's Palace. The imposing mass of the tower dates from Bishop Beauchamp's extensive reconstruction in about 1460 of the early medieval building. The drawing (left) is by Alexander Ansted and it comes from *Episcopal Palaces of England* of 1895, edited by Edmund Venables, Precentor of Lincoln Cathedral, who also wrote the section on Salisbury (95x60). Below is a more angled view by Joseph Pennell dated 1 August 1885, which comes from Mrs Schuyler Van Rensselaer's *English Cathedrals* of 1887 (95x135).

Two further views of the former Bishop's Palace by Alexander Ansted from *Episcopal Palaces of England* of 1895 edited by Edmund Venables. The one left is of the north front (60x110) and that below of the interior of the chapel (100x60).

The original early medieval former Bishop's Palace of the 1220s has undergone extensive alterations in most centuries since that date. Above is the earliest section and below a view from the terrace walk of the gardens. Both are by Alexander Ansted and come from *Episcopal Palaces of England* of 1895 edited by Edmund Venables (above 100x80; below 75x100).

Two very similar views of the former Bishop's Palace. The one above is by Nelly Erichsen from Edward Hutton's *Highways and Byways in Wiltshire* of 1917 (60x90). That below is by Charles E. Flower and comes from E.E. Dorling's *History of Salisbury* of 1911 (65x125).

Two attractive doorcases in the Close. On the left number 9 and on the right number 14. Both pencil drawings are by R. Grundy Heape from his *Salisbury – Some Architecture in the City and Close* of 1934 (number 9 125x100; number 14 150x100).

Number 21 The Close, a house called Aula le Stage or Tower House. The drawing is by J. Fisher and comes from Peter Hall's *Picturesque Memorials of Salisbury* of 1834, in which it is described as 'Canon Bowles House, an ecclesiastical mansion of great antiquity'. As the house originally dates from the thirteenth century, this seems a fair description (50x90).

Two houses in the Close on busy days with plenty of people and activity. Above is number 36 and below number 38. Both are sketches by R. Grundy Heape from his *Salisbury – Some Architecture in the City and Close* of 1934. The cars and dress of the period are prominent features and the College of Matrons appears to the left of number 38 (number 36 90x130; number 38 125x175).

A sketch and a measured drawing of the College of Matrons (number 39-46 the Close), founded by Bishop Seth Ward at his own expense in 1682 to house clergy widows. It was so extensively remodelled in 1870 by Thomas Henry Wyatt that it constituted almost a total rebuilding. The sketch is by Charles E. Flower from E.E. Dorling's *History of Salisbury* of 1911, while the measured drawing by Michael Bunney comes from *English Domestic Architecture of the Seventeenth and Eighteenth Centuries* by Horace Field and Michael Bunney of 1905 (sketch 75x90; measured drawing 140x112).

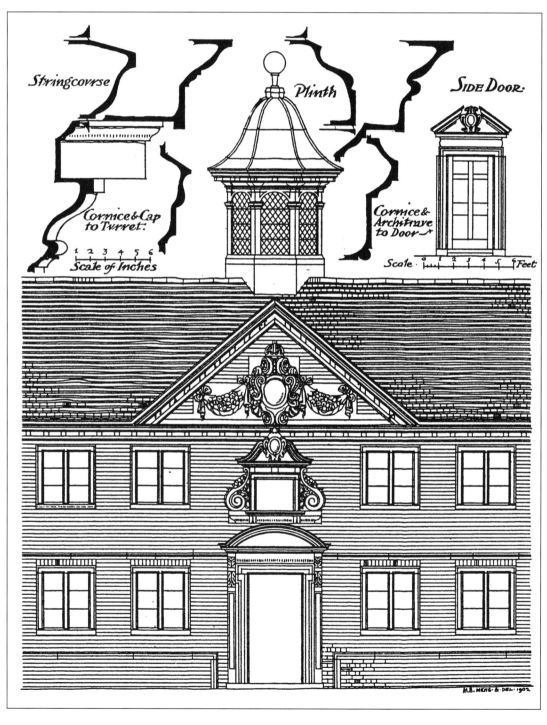

The College of Matrons sketched by R. Grundy Heape from his *Salisbury – Some Architecture in the City and Close* of 1934. The dress of the people passing by gives it a delightful period charm (135x175).

Until about 1900 number 48 the Close was the Porter's Lodge. It dates originally from the fourteenth century, but has undergone considerable alteration in the intervening period. This is also one of R. Grundy Heape's pencil drawings from his *Salisbury – Some Architecture in the City and Close* of 1934 (160x115).

Number 53 the Close is known as Mompesson House after owners during the seventeenth and early eighteenth centuries. The most famous member of the family was William, Rector of Eyam in Derbyshire, who proved to be a real shepherd to his flock when the village was decimated by the plague from September 1665 to October 1666. The house appears to be an amalgamation of several smaller buildings, which were refaced in the eighteenth century. Above one of R. Grundy Heape's drawings from his *Salisbury – Some Architecture in the City and Close* of 1934 (125x190). Below is a measured drawing by R. Shekleton Balfour of August 1894 from volume 2 of the *Third Series of the Architectural Association's Sketch Books* (270x380). The house is now owned by the National Trust.

Numbers 56a and 56b the Close were in fact originally one house called Hemyngsby, which appears to be a variation of the name of Canon Alexander Hemingby, who bequeathed the building to the Dean and Chapter in 1334. It was altered considerably in the second half of the seventeenth century and again in the early eighteenth century with some remodelling after the First World War. Finally it was made into two separate dwellings in 1950. Above is a view by J. Fisher in Peter Hall's *Picturesque Memorials of Salisbury* of 1834 (50x75) and below a sketch by R. Grundy Heape from his *Salisbury – Some Architecture in the City and Close* of exactly a century later (100x135).

Another view of Hemyngsby from the Choristers' Green with surrounding houses by R. Grundy Heape from his *Salisbury – Some Architecture in the City and Close* of 1934 (65x140).

Number 56 the Close, originally the Choristers' School, as seen in an engraving by John Chessel Buckler from his *Views of Sixty Endowed Grammar Schools* of 1827. The foundation was in 1717 and by 1980 this building had ceased to be used by the School (95x150).

An exterior and interior view of the Choristers' School from R. Grundy Heape's *Salisbury – Some Architecture in the City and Close* of 1934. The exterior has acquired a covering of foliage since John Chessel Buckler's engraved view and the interior shows the headmaster's desk in a handsomely panelled room, which even by the 1930s must have looked very old-fashioned (exterior 95x135; interior 130x175).

Number 58 the Close called the Wardrobe. It is a medieval building, which acquired its present name by 1543 and perhaps at that time was a household store for the Bishop. It had alterations in the sixteenth, seventeenth, eighteenth and nineteenth centuries and is now a military museum. The sketch dated 6 October 1900 is by Fred Roe and comes from P.H. Ditchfield's *Vanishing England* of 1910 (110x160).

Number 60 the Close is called the North Canonry, although it ceased to be a Canonry by 1940. It is a sixteenth century house within a thirteenth century shell, which has undergone a number of later restorations, especially one by Sir George Gilbert Scott in the late nineteenth century. This view is by J. Fisher from Peter Hall's *Picturesque Memorials of Salisbury* of 1834 (110x145).

Number 65 the Close is called the King's House as James I resided here when visiting Salisbury in 1610 and 1613. This extensive building is mainly of the fifteenth to the seventeenth century. In the nineteenth century it was used as a school and later as a training college for schoolmistresses, which necessitated considerable alterations to the fabric. From 1979 it has served as the Salisbury and South Wiltshire Museum. This view by J. Fisher is from Peter Hall's *Picturesque Memorials of Salisbury* of 1834 (95x160).

The porch of the King's House. This anonymous drawing comes from Peter Hall's *Picturesque Memorials of Salisbury* of 1834 (70x50).

A further view of the North Canonry featuring the entrance area. It is by R. Grundy Heape from his *Salisbury – Some Architecture in the City and Close* of 1934 (155x115).

Two further views of the King's House, this time by R. Grundy Heape in his *Salisbury – Some Architecture in the City and Close* of 1934. Very little seems to have changed in the intervening century following J. Fisher's drawing on the previous page (above general view 130x180; left detail of the windows 170x130).

Two drawings by R. Grundy Heape from his *Salisbury – Some Architecture in the City and Close* of 1934. Above number 68 the Close, a handsome eighteenth century house built on the site of a medieval canonry with elegant internal decoration (115x135). Below number 69 the Close known as the Walton Canonry after Canon Isaac Walton, a son of the famous writer and fishing enthusiast. Canon Isaac Walton was in occupation from 1698 to 1719 and in 1720 the present house was constructed with nineteenth century alterations and modifications in 1960 to create a chapel for Bishop Pike of Sherborne (115x140).

Part of the Close wall with the tower and spire of the Cathedral in the background. The sketch is by Charles E. Flower from E.E. Dorling's *History of Salisbury* of 1911 (75x85).

A drawing by Joseph Pennell from Mrs Schuyler Van Rensselaer's *English Cathedrals* of 1887. The actual date of the view is 28 July 1885 and there is an air of spaciousness about this high summer's day with houses in the Close and part of the west front of the Cathedral (80x130).

OTHER CHURCHES

Compared with the City of London or a place like Norwich, Salisbury has remarkably few original parish churches. St Martin's at the east end of the City served a settlement, which had preceded the main development and is now effectively cut off from it by Churchill Way East. It is originally of the thirteenth century with later alterations and Victorian restoration. St Thomas of Canterbury overlooks the market place and has always been the church of the rich merchants of the area. It is fifteenth century and later, as the chancel collapsed in 1447 and rebuilding followed soon afterwards. St Edmund is largely perpendicular except for the seventeenth century west tower and Victorian work by Sir George Gilbert Scott. In 1973 it was declared redundant and is now an arts centre. St Andrew, Bemerton, was originally decorated but has been heavily restored, while St John, Bemerton, is a memorial church to George Herbert, who was Rector from 1630 to 1632. The building of

1861 was designed by Thomas Henry Wyatt and has the air of a church in the grounds of a great house.

St Clement's church at Fisherton was demolished in 1852 and replaced in the same year by the present St Paul's. St George's, Harnham, has a chancel and nave of the early twelfth century with fourteenth century alterations and was restored by William Butterfield in 1873. The Catholic church of St Osmund in Exeter Street of 1847-1848 was designed by Augustus Welby Pugin, the Baptist church in Brown Street is of 1829, the United Reformed church, Fisherton Street of 1879 is by Tarring and Wilkinson and the Methodist church, St Edmund Street, is of 1810-1811 with later additions. There is one church of note in the period between the two World Wars, St Francis in Castle Road of 1936-1939 by Robert Potter, while the post-Second World War era is represented by St Michael, North Bemerton of 1956-1957 by N.F. Cachemaille-Day.

St Martin's church is on the east side of Salisbury with a chancel dating from the first half of the thirteenth century and the tower from the early fourteenth century. Further work was done in succeeding centuries culminating in an extensive restoration in 1886. This view by J. Fisher shows the sexton digging a grave while talking to the woman with a child clinging to her skirts. The drawing comes from Peter Hall's *Picturesque Memorials of Salisbury* of 1834 (120x175).

A drawing of St Martin's church by Charles E. Flower from E.E. Dorling's *History of Salisbury* of 1911. The tower, spire and west end of the building feature strongly in this view (105x70).

An anonymous sketch of the font in St Martin's church. It comes from Peter Hall's *Picturesque Memorials of Salisbury* of 1834 (55x50).

The church of St Thomas of Canterbury stands in the square named after it and overlooks the market. It was always the church of the City's rich merchants and when the chancel collapsed in 1447 it was quickly rebuilt. As befits a church of this status this was done in grand style as the beautiful low pitched interior roof testifies. The tower dates from between 1400 and 1405 and was originally detached from the main building. Some of the interior furnishings are eighteenth century, while the reredos of 1868 and the pulpit of 1876 are by George Edmund Street. There is also a heavily restored Doom over the Chancel arch. The sketch above is by Nelly Erichsen from Edward Hutton's *Highways and Byways in Wiltshire* of 1917 (110x90), while that right is by Charles E. Flower from E.E. Dorling's *History of Salisbury* of 1911 (85x75).

Above is a view of St Thomas' church from the River Avon drawn and engraved by J. Fisher. It comes from Peter Hall's *Picturesque Memorials of Salisbury* of 1834 (105x140). Right is a drawing from the same source showing the interior of St Thomas' church with the then existing box pews and part of the fine roof (165x115).

The church of St Edmund in Bedwin Street, which was declared redundant in 1973 and is now an arts centre. It is almost completely perpendicular in style except for the west tower rebuilt in 1653-1655 and additions by Sir George Gilbert Scott of 1865-1867. This unsigned drawing is presumably by J. Fisher and comes from Peter Hall's *Picturesque Memorials of Salisbury* of 1834 (110x175).

St Clement's church, Fisherton, is shown in this view by J. Fisher from Peter Hall's *Picturesque Memorials of Salisbury* of 1834. The building was demolished in 1852, but some of the fittings were transferred to St. Paul's Church, which was built in the same year, but 350 yards to the north (110x165).

The two churches of Bemerton. That (left) is the original heavily restored parish church with a pretty tile hung bell turret. The drawing is by Nelly Erichsen and comes from Edward Hutton's *Highways and Byways in Wiltshire* of 1917 (65x90). The one below is the memorial church to George Herbert, the noted poet and hymn writer, who was Rector here from 1630 to 1632. The architect of this memorial church of 1861 is Thomas Henry Wyatt and it was constructed at the expense of the Pembrokes of Wilton. The drawing comes from the *Builder* of 20 April 1861 and is by J. Casgoine with the wood engraving by W.E. Hodckin (150x170).

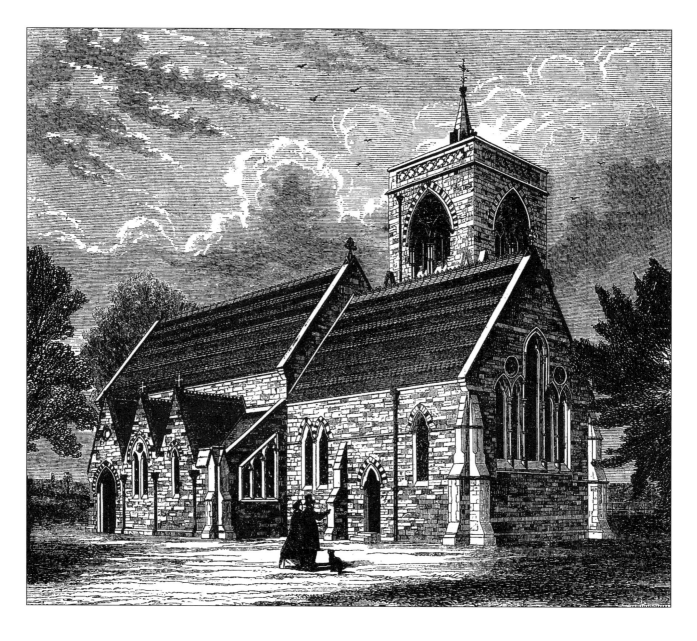

ACKNOWLEDGEMENTS

The advice and assistance of a number of people is always needed in writing a book of this kind and I would like to acknowledge with grateful thanks help from the following people and institutions; the Society of Antiquaries for permission to reproduce material and especially the Librarian Bernard Nurse and his staff in meeting my requirements for books, housed in rather distant and obscure parts of the Society's premises; the courteous staffs of the London Library and the City of London's Guildhall Library; my wife Marion for her expert advice as an architectural historian; Steven Pugsley and his staff at Halsgrove Publishing for general encouragement in compilation; and finally, but not least, a special thanks to all those artists and engravers, long since gathered to their fathers, whose skills shine through these pages in bringing the past of the City of Salisbury so vividly alive.

Stratford sub Castle lies immediately below Old Sarum to the west beside the River Avon. This view of 1832 is by J. Fisher and includes the manor house and St Lawrence church. It comes from Peter Hall's *Picturesque Memorials of Salisbury* of 1834 (110x175).

SUGGESTIONS FOR FURTHER READING

Alarge number of books and periodicals are mentioned in the body of the text and it seems pointless to repeat them here, except for John Britton's *Cathedral Antiquities* (1814) and Francis Price's *A Series of Observations on the Cathedral Church of Salisbury* (1753, but reprinted in 1997). The former has a detailed account of James Wyatt's work in the 1790s and the latter, by the then surveyor to the Cathedral, is a highly competent structural report in the mid-eighteenth century before Wyatt's alterations.

For any proper understanding of the City, the three volumes of the *Royal Commission on Historical Monuments* are essential reading. Volume one (1980) covers the City in general and further volumes on the architectural history of the Cathedral and on the Close followed in 1993. There are two volumes to come on specialist aspects of the Cathedral, one of the monuments and stained glass and the other on the tower and spire. Although an older publication, volume 6 of the *Victoria County History of Wiltshire* (1962) covers Salisbury and is still a useful reference work.

For biographical information in general the *Dictionary of National Biography* and *Who Was Who* are essential. More specialist works I have found useful are Simon Houfe's *Dictionary of Nineteenth Century Illustrators* (revised edition 1996) and Ronald Russell's *Guide to Topographical Prints* (1979), but above all Bernard Adams' *London Illustrated 1604-1851* (1983). This outstanding work of scholarship deals not only with exclusively London material, but also publications covering the whole country that have London sections, and

therefore includes a mass of useful detail about artists and engravers found in the present volume.

For early architects Michael Hicks' *Who's Who in Late Medieval England 1272-1485* (1991) and John Harvey's *English Medieval Architects – A Biographical Dictionary* (1984) are helpful. For later architects, Sir Howard Colvin's *Dictionary of British Architects 1600-1840* (third edition 1995) is indispensable and the *Dictionary of British Architects 1834-1900* (1993) brings the story up to the end of the nineteenth century. The extremely helpful Wiltshire volume of the *Buildings of England* series edited by Sir Nikolaus Pevsner, originally of 1963, was revised by Bridget Cherry in 1975, and apart from its detailed architectural descriptions of Salisbury buildings, is particularly good on its suggested perambulations around the streets of the City centre.

There are naturally a number of books of a more general nature covering Salisbury alone. Although produced half a century ago, two mainly photographic studies of the Cathedral still have a timeless relevance. They are G.H. Cook's *Portrait of Salisbury Cathedral* (1950) and Jeffrey Truby's *Glories of Salisbury Cathedral* (1948). Hugh Scott's *City of Salisbury* (1957) concludes with a good bibliography and the same is even more true of John Chandler's *Endless Street* (1983). Also still readable are H.L.P. Jowitt's *Salisbury* (1951) and Ralph Whitlock's *Salisbury Plain* (1955). Thomas Sharp's *New Sarum – A Plan for Salisbury* (1949) was published in the post-war flush of enthusiasm for town planning and it is interesting to compare the concepts and suggestions with the reality of fifty years later.

Two stone ornaments from the arcade round the Cathedral chapter house. The artist is James Kellaway Colling and they come from volume two of his work entitled *Gothic Ornaments* of 1850. The lithographer is J.R. Jobbins and the date of these particular illustrations 1 September 1848 (each 90x115).